Outline of Hinduism

William Stoddart

The illustration on the cover (an 18th century Kangra miniature) is of Krishna, the 8th Incarnation of Vishnu, and His Consort Radha (see page 23).

In Christianity, the intensity of Divine Love is symbolized by the familiar image of the Madonna and Child; in Hinduism, on the other hand, the less familiar image of the mutual love of man and woman symbolizes the same Divine Reality (see pages 33-34). Maternal love, conjugal love, Divine Love: the first two are both images of the third.

Published by
The Foundation for Traditional Studies

For information, address
The Foundation for Traditional Studies
1633 Q Street, NW
Washington, D.C. 20009

Library of Congress Catalog Card Number: 92-74413

ISBN: 0-9629984-1-9

Contents

iv

v

Illustrations

Acknowledgements

The author wishes to thank Shri Keshavram Iengar of Mysore for permission to reproduce his Sanscrit calligraphy on page 61 and also for much help and information.

He also wishes to thank Monsieur Dominique Wohlschlag of Confignon, Switzerland, for his expert guidance regarding the transliteration of Sanscrit words.

The sketches of the Hindu Gods on pages 24-25 were taken from *A Handbook to India, Pakistan, Burma and Ceylon* (John Murray, London, 1962) edited by Professor L. F. Rushbrook Williams, C.B.E. and Sir Arthur C. Lothian, K.C.I.E.

The sketches of the incarnations of Vishnu on page 29 were taken from a publication of the Indian Students Association of Manchester, England, in the 1950s.

Thanks are due to Perennial Books, Bedfont, England and Quinta Essentia, Cambridge, England for permission to reproduce extracts from the writings of Frithjof Schuon and Titus Burckhardt.

Design on title-page by courtesy of Abodes Inc.

Lead me from the unreal to the Real;
Lead me from darkness to Light;
Lead me from death to Immortality.

Brihadâranyaka Upanishad, I, 3, 27.

(1) What is religion?

In terms of etymology, religion is that which binds, specifically, that which binds man to God. Religion engages man in two ways: firstly, by explaining the nature and meaning of the universe, or "justifying the ways of God to man" (this is theodicy); and secondly, by elucidating man's role and purpose in the universe, or teaching him how to liberate himself from its limitations, constrictions and terrors (this is soteriology).

In the first place, religion is a *doctrine* of unity: God, who is both Creator and Final End of the universe and of man in it, is one. In the second place, religion is a *method* of union: a sacramental path, a way of return, a means of salvation.

Whatever they may be called, these two components are always present: theodicy and soteriology; doctrine and method; theory and practice; dogma and sacrament; unity and union.

Doctrine, or theory, concerns the mind; method, or practice, concerns the will. Religion, to be itself, must always engage both mind and will.

The second, or practical, component of religion may be broken into two: namely, worship and morality. Worship, the sacramental element, generally takes the form of participation in the revealed rites (public or private) of a given religion, the purpose being the assimilation of man's will to that of God.

Morality, the social element, is "doing the things which ought to be done, and not doing the things which ought not to be done". Some of the contents of morality are universal: "thou shalt not bear false witness", "thou shalt not kill", "thou shalt not steal", etc.; and some of the contents are specific to the religion in question: "thou shalt not make a graven image", "whom God hath joined together, let no man put asunder", etc.

We have thus reached the three elements which René Guénon considered to be the defining features of every religion: dogma, worship, and morality. When raised to a higher or more intense degree, namely that of spirituality or mysticism, they become, in the words of Frithjof Schuon: truth, spiritual way, and virtue.

*
* *

The most important single point about religion is that it is not man-made. Religion is not invented by man, but revealed by God. Divine revelation is a *sine quâ non*; without it, there is no religion, only man-made ideology, in which no sacramental or salvational element is present.

The next important fundamental is tradition. Having once been revealed, religion is then handed down — unchanged in essence, but often increasingly elaborated in expression — from one generation to the next, by the power of tradition. And finally, closely linked with tradition, comes the attribute of orthodoxy, which is viewed as the principle of truth, or, at the practical level, the preservation of doctrinal purity.

In summary: religion's essential contents comprise dogma, worship, and morality; and religion's indispensable "container" or framework comprises revelation, tradition, and orthodoxy.

I am seated in the hearts of all.

Bhagavad-Gîtâ, XV, 15.

(2) What is orthodoxy?

Nowadays, more often than not, orthodoxy is considered to be simply a form of intolerance: one set of people imposing their own views on others. In this connection, however, it is useful to recall the first item on the "Noble Eightfold Path" of Buddhism: this is "right views" or "right thinking". It is obvious why "right thinking" should enjoy pride of place, for, both logically and practically, it is prior to "right doing". And what is the English word (derived from Greek) that signifies "right thinking"? None other than "orthodoxy".

To take the matter further: $2 + 2 = 4$ is orthodox; $2 + 2 = 5$ is unorthodox. Rather simple — but it also works the same way at much loftier levels. Another way of looking at it is this: even in the circumstances of today, many people still preserve the notion of "moral purity", and lay high value on it. Orthodoxy is "intellectual purity", and as such is an indispensable prelude to grace. Seen in this way — and far from "telling people what to believe" — orthodoxy is no more than a reference to the primacy and priority of truth. Orthodoxy, indeed, is the principle of truth that runs through the myths, symbols and dogmas which are the very language of revelation.

Like morality, orthodoxy may be either universal (conformity to truth as such) or specific (conformity to the forms of a given religion). It is universal when it declares that God is uncreated, or that God is absolute and infinite. It is specific when it declares that Jesus is God (Christianity), or that God takes the triple form of Brahmâ, Vishnu, and Shiva (Hinduism).

Departure from orthodoxy is heresy: either intrinsic (for example, atheism), or extrinsic (for example, a Muslim not believing in the divinity of Jesus).

Orthodoxy is normal, heresy abnormal. This permits the use of a medical metaphor: the study of the various traditional orthodoxies is the affair of the religious physiologist, whereas the study of heresies (were it worthwhile) is the affair of the religious pathologist.

Orthodoxy is particularly important in a world in which the great religions have become conscious of one another, and whose adherents often live cheek by jowl. It is similarly important in the field of comparative religion. This point has been well expressed by Bernard Kelly:

> "Confusion is inevitable whenever cultures based on profoundly different spiritual traditions intermingle without rigid safeguards to preserve their purity. The crusader with the cross emblazoned on his breast, the loincloth and spindle of Mahatma Gandhi when he visited Europe, are images of the kind of precaution that is reasonable when traveling in a spiritually alien territory. The modern traveler in his bowler hat and pin stripes is safeguarded by that costume against any lack of seriousness in discussing finance. Of more important safeguards he knows

nothing. The complete secularism of the modern Western world, wherever its influence has spread, has opened the floodgates to a confusion which sweeps away the contours of the spirit.... Traditional norms ... provide the criteria of culture and civilization. Traditional orthodoxy is thus the pre-requisite of any discourse at all between the traditions themselves.'"

'*Dominican Studies* (London), volume 7, 1954, page 256.

Sages call the One Reality by many names.

Rig Veda, I, 164, 46.

(3) The place of Hinduism
amongst the religions of the world

The religions of the world fall naturally into three broad categories: the Hyperborean shamanisms (which include Confucianism, Taoism, Shinto, and the religion of the North American Indians), the Aryan mythologies (which include Hinduism, Buddhism, and the extinct Greco-Roman religion), and the Semitic monotheisms (comprising Judaism, Christianity, and Islam).

It is an aid to the understanding of Hinduism to recall that it is cognate with the religion of ancient Greece. Both religions are Aryan (the Hindu sacred language Sanscrit and the Greek language are related); both are mythological (their pantheons are analogous: the Supreme Being in Hinduism is Ishvara, in Greece Zeus); the popular (or exoteric) religion in both cases finds expression in epics (the *Râmâyana* and the *Mahâbhârata* in Hinduism, the *Iliad* and the *Odyssey* in Greece); the wisdom-systems (or esoterisms) are analogous (Vedânta in Hinduism, Pythagorism and Platonism in Greece); the temple architectures (column-and-lintel construction; stepped-roof construction) are analogous. (Contrast the Roman, Christian, and Islamic arch — derived ultimately from the Etruscan arch.)

Quite a different story is the contrast observable between Hinduism and the Semitic monotheisms, particularly Islam. One is Aryan, the other Semitic; one is mythological (and "polytheistic"), the other theological (and monotheistic); one is hierarchical, the other "egalitarian" (not in any modern sense, however); the writing of the one goes from left to right, that of the other from right to left; in circumambulatory rites, the Hindu motion is clockwise, the Islamic anti-clockwise; upper-class Hindu women (in classical times) could properly be semi-nude, while Muslim women (especially upper-class) are completely enshrouded; Hindus (in the main) are vegetarian (the only entire people in the world to be so), while Muslims are meat-eaters; Hinduism is the oldest of the religions, Islam the youngest: there is something primordial about Hinduism, and something of the nature of the latter days about Islam.

It is very remarkable, and surely providential, that two divine revelations as distinct from one another as Hinduism and Islam should exist side-by-side in the land of India. Speaking of the respective spiritualities, Dârâ Shukûh, the son of the Mughal emperor Shâh Jahân, declared: "The science of Sufism and the science of Vedânta are one." Or, as Gandhi succinctly put it: *Îshvara Allâh Tere Nam* ("*Îshvara* and *Allâh*, both are Thy Names").

The classification of the main world religions is shown schematically on the facing page:

Classification of the Religions

I. The Hyperborean Shamanisms

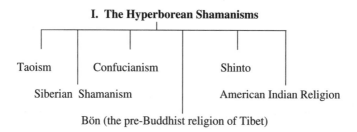

Taoism   Confucianism   Shinto

Siberian Shamanism   American Indian Religion

Bön (the pre-Buddhist religion of Tibet)

II. The Aryan Mythologies

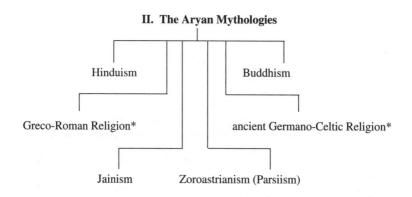

Hinduism   Buddhism

Greco-Roman Religion*   ancient Germano-Celtic Religion*

Jainism   Zoroastrianism (Parsiism)

extinct

III. The Semitic Monotheisms

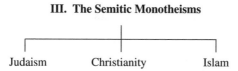

Judaism   Christianity   Islam

North Indian Temple
(The Jagannath Temple at Puri)

(4) The religion of a people

When use is made of the expression "world religions", it is important to be aware of the distinction between those religions which address their message to "all nations", and those whose message is restricted to virtually one people. In the former category are the "missionary" religions Buddhism, Christianity and Islam, which may properly be designated as "universal", which preach to everyone, and which have adherents in many lands. In the latter category are Hinduism and Judaism, which are not missionary, and which, broadly speaking, are the religions of one people or one nation only.

Buddhism, Christianity and Islam, all accept, and often strongly seek, converts. Hinduism and Judaism, on the other hand — no doubt with certain very special exceptions — do not seek, nor do they normally accept, converts. In general, in order to be a member of one of these religions, it is necessary to be born into it; specifically, in the case of Hinduism, it is also a question of being born into a caste (see page 43).

Anyone can become a Buddhist, a Christian, or a Muslim, but one must be born a Hindu.

The term "Hinduism" is generally accepted as an accurate and suitable one for the religion we are studying but, in the Hindu tradition itself, it is often referred to as the *Sanâtana Dharma* (the "Perennial Law" or "Primordial Norm").

In what is night for the ignorant, the sage is awake;
in what is night for the sage, the ignorant are awake.

Bhagavad-Gîtâ, II, 69.

(5) Elements of Hindu metaphysics

In Hinduism, the Supreme Principle, absolute and infinite, is *Brahma* (or *Brahman*). The first self-determination of *Brahma* is *Îshvara* (the personal God). The world or universe (*samsara* or *jagat*) is an emanation or manifestation of *Îshvara* (who nevertheless remains transcendent with regard to it).

In the metaphysical terminology of Guénon and Schuon, the correspondences are as follows:

Brahma nirguna ("*Brahma* unqualified")	=	Beyond-Being (the Divine Essence)
Brahma saguna ("*Brahma* qualified" or *Îshvara*)	=	Being (the Personal God)
samsâra (or *jagat*)	=	existence, manifestation, or creation

Two terms are applied to the Supreme Principle: *Brahma* and *Âtmâ*. Both are conceived as transcendent and immanent, but the idea of transcendence attaches more to *Brahma*, and the idea of immanence attaches more to *Âtmâ*.

Para-Brahma (the "supreme Brahma") corresponds to *Brahma nirguna* ("*Brahma* unqualified"). *Apara-Brahma* (the "non-supreme *Brahma*" corresponds to *Brahma saguna* ("*Brahma* qualified" or *Îshvara*).

Âtmâ can likewise be conceived at these two levels: *Paramâtmâ* (the "supreme Self") and *Âtmâ* (the "non-supreme Self", that is, at the level of the Personal God).

Everything beneath the level of *Brahma nirguna* or *Para-Brahma* pertains to the realm of *mâyâ* (the "non-absolute" or "relative"). The concept of *mâyâ* thus includes both *Îshvara* and *samsâra*, Being and existence, Creator and creation. Only "Beyond-Being" (the Divine Essence) is Absolute. The level of "Being" may be regarded, in the words of Frithjof Schuon, as "relatively Absolute". (See also pages 37-38.)

In Hinduism, it is said: "The world is false (unreal), *Brahma* is true (real)." This expresses the exclusiveness of the Supreme Principle, and the ultimate unreality of all that "is not".

It is also said: "All things (in their ultimate and permanent essence) are *Âtmâ*." This expresses the inclusiveness of the Supreme Principle, and the ultimate reality of all that "is".

Âtmâ (in the sense of *Paramâtmâ*, the Absolute) is often used to mean "the True" (or "the Real"). *Mâyâ* (which is the relative) is often used to mean "the false" (or "the illusory"). However, *mâyâ* can also be viewed positively as *Krishna-Lîlâ*: "divine play", "divine art", "divine magic", or "appearance".

In the process towards manifestation, Being (*Îshvara*) is polarized into an active or male principle, *Purusha*, and a passive or female principle, *Prakriti*. From the interaction of these two parental principles, existence or manifestation (*samsâra* or *jagat*) is born. See also section (9) (pages 33-34).

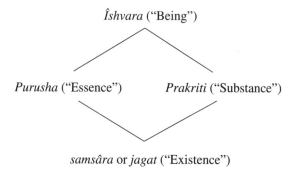

Îshvara ("Being")

Purusha ("Essence")   *Prakriti* ("Substance")

samsâra or *jagat* ("Existence")

The sacred monosyllable *OM* (see title page) is regarded as being identical with *Âtmâ* and *Brahma*. It is composed of three letters, *A*, *U*, and *M*, the first two contracting into *O*. As the vehicle of Divinity, the sacred monosyllable is frequently invoked by Hindus, generally accompanying another revealed Name of God.

Brahma satyam, jagan mithyâ.
God is Reality, the world is appearance.

(6) The two Trinities of Hinduism

In Hinduism, there are two great Trinities, one of which may be called "horizontal", and the other "vertical".

Mythologically — that is to say, in terms of the Hindu pantheon — *Îshvara* ("Being", or the Personal God) is seen as having three aspects (*Trimûrti* = the triple manifestation). These are *Brahmâ*, the Creator, *Vishnu*, the Preserver, and *Shiva*, the Destroyer or Transformer. This constitutes the "horizontal" Trinity:

Brahmâ ——— **Vishnu** ——— **Shiva**
(Creator)   (Preserver)   (Destroyer or
                                         Transformer)

Note

One must take care to distinguish between *Brahma* (or *Brahman*), the Supreme Principle, and *Brahmâ*, the first of the three aspects or "Faces" of *Îshvara*.

The "vertical" Trinity is constituted by *Sat-Chit-Ânanda* (*Sachchidânanda*), the three internal dimensions or hypostases of the Supreme Principle, Brahma:

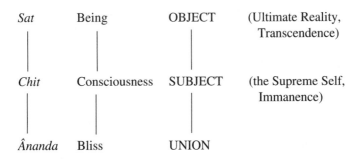

Sat	Being	OBJECT	(Ultimate Reality, Transcendence)
Chit	Consciousness	SUBJECT	(the Supreme Self, Immanence)
Ânanda	Bliss	UNION	

René Guénon has pointed out how the "vertical" Trinity of Hinduism (Being-Consciousness-Bliss) stands in an analogical relationship to the Trinity of Christianity (Father, Son, and Holy-Spirit). This is particularly apparent when one recalls St.-Augustine's designation of the Christian Trinity as "Being-Wisdom-Life".

For the "operative" or "spiritual" application of the doctrine of *Sat-Chit-Ânanda*, see page 58.

(7) The Hindu Pantheon

It was indicated on pages 9 and 10 that the Hindu and Greco-Roman religions are cognate, and attention was drawn to the various analogies between them. The Greco-Roman pantheon is more or less well known, the Hindu pantheon less so. The following few pages contain summary and schematic outlines of the main members of the Hindu pantheon, under the headings of the Vedic Gods, the Puranic Gods, and the Incarnations (*Avatâras*) of Vishnu.

I. The Vedic Gods

The ancient Vedic Gods have been classified in a variety of ways.

The Sovereigns
Mitra
Varuna

The Fighters
Indra
Rudra

The Gods of Fertility
Aditi
Agni

Eight of the Vedic Gods are known as "the Guardians of the Eight Quarters":

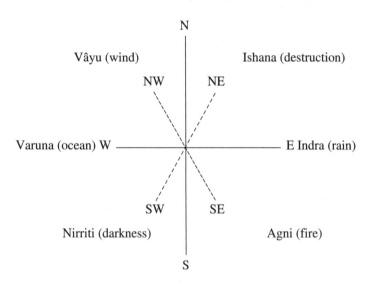

Kubera (wealth)

Vâyu (wind)   Ishana (destruction)

Varuna (ocean)   Indra (rain)

Nirriti (darkness)   Agni (fire)

Yama (death)

Amongst the Vedic Gods are:

Aditi (Infinity; Mother of the Gods)
Kama (love)
Sürya (sun)
Chandra (moon)
Rudra (storms)

II. The Puranic Gods

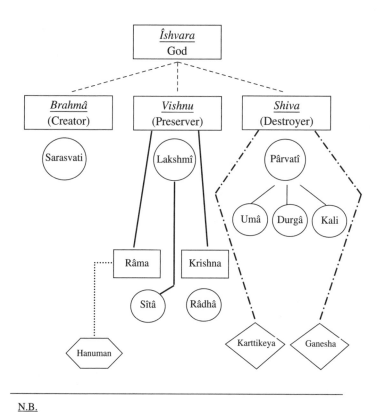

<u>N.B.</u>

Râma and Krishna are two of the ten Incarnations (*Avatâras*) of Vishnu.

▭	Gods	- - - - - - - - -	Hypostases
◯	Consorts (*Shaktis*)	————————	Incarnations or Manifestations
◇	Sons	— · — · — · —	Sons
⬡	helper	··················	helper

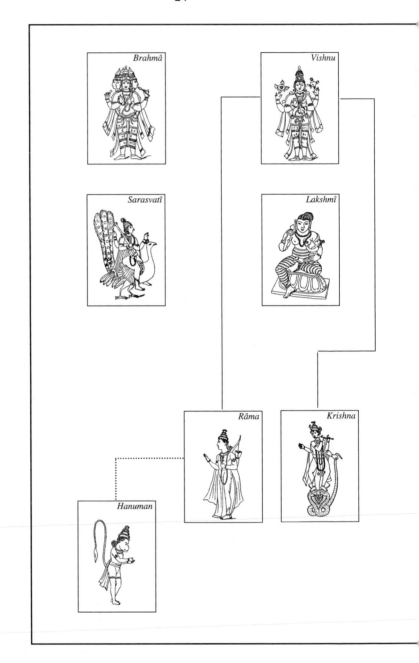

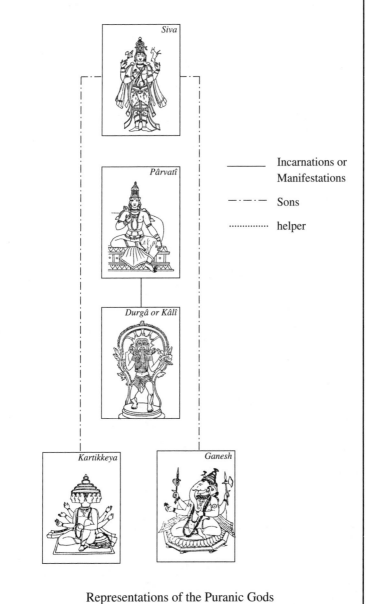

Representations of the Puranic Gods

*Vidagdha Shâkalya asked: "How many gods are there,
O Yâjñavalkya?"*
*He replied: "As many as are mentioned in the hymn to the
Vishvedevas, namely, three and three hundred, three and three
thousand."*
*"Yes," he said, and asked again: "How many gods are there really,
O Yâjñavalkya?"*
"Thirty-three," he said.
*"Yes," he said, and asked again: "How many gods are there really,
O Yâjñavalkya?"*
"Six," he said.
*"Yes", he said, and asked again: "How many gods are there really,
O Yâjñavalkya?"*
"Three," he said.
*"Yes," he said, and asked again: "How many gods are there really,
O Yâjñavalkya?"*
"Two," he said.
*"Yes," he said, and asked again: "How many gods are there really,
O Yâjñavalkya?"*
"One and a half," he said.
*"Yes", he said, and asked again: "How many gods are there really,
O Yâjñavalkya?"*
"One," he said.

*Then Vidagdha Shâkalya asked: "Who are these three and three
hundred, three and three thousand?"*
Yâjñavalkya replied: "These are only the various powers."

Brihadâranyaka Upanishad, III, 9, 1.

III. The Incarnations of Vishnu

Whenever the Law* is forgotten,
whenever anarchy prevails,
I incarnate Myself.

In every age I come back:
to deliver the righteous,
to destroy the wicked,
to establish the Law.

Bhagavad-Gîtâ, IV, 7-8.

Unlike Judaism and Islam, but like Buddhism and Christianity, Hinduism is "incarnationist". This is seen above all in the ten Incarnations (*Avatâras*) of Vishnu, which have successively appeared on earth for the salvation of men. There have already been nine such Incarnations, and a tenth is expected — at the end of the world.

The ten Incarnations (*Avatâras*) of *Vishnu* are shown overleaf:

---

*Dharma = Law, Norm.

(1) *Matsya*	Fish
(2) *Kûrma*	Tortoise
(3) *Varâha*	Boar
(4) *Narasimha*	Lion
(5) *Vâmana*	Dwarf
(6) *(Parashu) Râma*	(son of Bhrigumuni)
(7) *(Kodanda) Râma*	(son of Dasharatha) hero of the *Râmâyana*
(8) *Krishna*	hero of the *Mahâbhârata*
(9) *Buddha*	the *Buddha* as seen from *within* Hinduism
(10) *Kalki*	the Incarnation to come

The Buddha was not merely the Founder of Buddhism (which, as a new and original revelation emerging from the Hindu world, mediated the wisdom of the *Veda* to the whole of eastern Asia), but also appears within Hinduism as the ninth Incarnation of *Vishnu.*

The *Kalki-Avatâra* is expected to appear at the end of time. A similar apocalyptic expectation also exists in Christianity and Islam in the form of the second coming of Christ, and in Buddhism in the form of *Maitreya-Buddha.*

(1) **Mathsya** (Fish)

(2) **Kûrma** (Tortoise)

(3) **Varâha** (Boar)

(4) **Narasimha** (Lion)

(5) **Vâmana** (Dwarf)

(6) **(Parashu) Râma**

(7) **(Kodanda) Râma**

(8) **Krishna**

(9) **Buddha**

(10) **Kalki**

The ten Incarnations (*Avatâras*) of Vishnu

Vishnu
(South Indian, 10th century,
Metropolitan Museum of Art, New York)

(8) Incarnationism and iconodulia

In Hinduism, again as in Buddhism and Christianity, "incarnationism" is accompanied by a didactic and sacramental iconography. Judaism and Islam, to which incarnationism is foreign, are "iconoclastic" or "aniconic", whereas Hinduism, Buddhism and Christianity are "iconodulic". In Buddhism, there is the image of the Buddha; in Christianity, there are the icons of Christ, the Virgin, and the saints; in Hinduism, the Puranic Gods and the Incarnations of Vishnu often find expression in statues and paintings, as well as in sacred dance. Such images both teach and serve as vehicles for divine worship.

Completely renouncing all dharmas, seek Me alone as refuge. I shall release you from all sins.

Bhagavad-Gîtâ, XVIII, 66.

(9) Masculine and feminine principles

What might be called the feminine side of the Divine Economy is represented in Christianity by the Virgin Mary — "full of grace", according to the salutation of Gabriel, and "blessed amongst women", according to her cousin Elizabeth.

In Hinduism, the feminine presence is strong, and appears in the form of the "Consorts" (*Shaktis*) of the various Hypostases or Manifestations of God. (See pages 23-25.)

In the *Upanishads*, the Supreme *Brahma* is described as "That on which the universe is woven, as warp and weft". This symbolism of weaving is particularly suited for making clear the roles of the universal masculine and feminine principles *Purusha* and *Prakriti* (see page 17): the warp of the universe (and all things in it) is *Purusha*, and the weft is *Prakriti*. When, as is sometimes done, the God *Vishnu* and his Consort *Lakshmî* are taken to represent respectively the masculine and feminine principles, then the warp is *Vishnu* and the weft is *Lakshmî*.

This symbolism was pursued by the renowned weaver Aristide Messinesi, who was imbued with Gandhi's notion of *khadi* ("hand-spinning") when he spent some time in the latter's *âshram* at Wardha. Messinesi describes the shuttle of the horizontal hand-loom as "that elegant and charming creature, which can hardly be called an implement, so nearly does it come to possessing a life of its own". He continues:

> "Carrying the weft, it darts in and out of the warp, like a streak of lightning, or an arrow speeding to its mark; like a ship, it plies from shore to shore, out and home again; like *Lakshmî* casting flowers in *Vishnu*'s lap, it adorns and nourishes its Lord."

(From "A Craft as a Fountain of Grace and a Means of Realization" in *Art and Thought*, a *Festschrift* in honor of Ananda Coomaraswamy, Luzac, London, 1947.)

One mother is more venerable than a thousand fathers.

Mânava-Dharma-Shâstra, II, 145.

Shiva and Pârvatî
(Bronze statue, 11th century, privately owned, Basle)

(10) The Five Levels of Reality

(1)   *Âtmâ*:   the Divine Essence   "Beyond-Being"

(2)   *Îshvara*:   the Personal God   "Being"

(3)   *Buddhi*:   Spirit or Intellect   SPIRITUS,
                                                              INTELLECTUS

(4) ⎡─ *manas*   mind ─┐
       ⎢   ├─soul   ANIMA
       ⎣─ *prâna*   emotions ─┘

(5)   *sthûla*   body, sensations   CORPUS

     The first two levels pertain to God, the last three pertain to man. The last two levels are formal or individual; the middle level, *Buddhi* (Spirit or Intellect), although "created", is supra-formal, supra-individual or universal.

The middle level, *Buddhi* (Spirit or Intellect) is the created Logos; the second level, *Îshvara* (the Personal God) is the uncreated Logos.

Following the metaphysical exposition of Frithjof Schuon (see pages 15 and 16), one can say that the uncreated Logos is the prefiguration of the relative in the Absolute, and the created Logos is the reflection of the Absolute in the relative. In other words, *Îshvara* is *mâyâ* in *Âtmâ*, and *Buddhi* is *Âtmâ* in *mâyâ*.

It is the Logos, with its two "degrees", that constitutes the bridge between the created and the uncreated; it is thanks to the Logos that contact between man and God is possible.

A human being is known as a *jîvâtmâ* ("a being in this life"; *jîva* = life). *Vedânta* teaches how *Âtmâ*, manifesting itself in a *jîvâtmâ*, clothes itself in a series of five "envelopes" (*koshas*), representing different levels of manifestation. These five "envelopes" are listed below. The numbers have been adjusted to correspond with those on page 37.

(2) *ânanda-maya-kosha* = level of *Îshvara*   the Personal God

(3) *vijñâna-maya-kosha* = level of *Buddhi*   SPIRITUS, INTELLECTUS

(4a) *mano-maya-kosha* = mind ⌐

                                      — ANIMA

(4b) *prâna-maya-kosha* = vital breath ⌐

(5) *anna-maya-kosha* = nutriment, physical body   CORPUS

In addition to the scheme on the preceding page, there are also the three "forms" (*sharîras*) of man. These are shown hereunder. The numbers have been adjusted to correspond with those on page 37.

(3) *kârana-sharîra* = Spirit or Intellect SPIRITUS,
                                      (supra-formal INTELLECTUS
                                      or universal)

(4) *sukshma-sharîra* = mind and feeling ANIMA
                                      (individual:
                                      subtle form)

(5) *sthûla-sharîra* = body CORPUS
                                        (individual:
                                        gross form)

(11) Hindu cosmology

**The three *gunas* ("cosmic tendencies")
and the five *bhûtas* ("corporeal manifestations")**

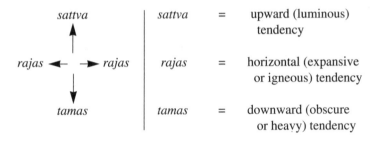

sattva	=	upward (luminous) tendency
rajas	=	horizontal (expansive or igneous) tendency
tamas	=	downward (obscure or heavy) tendency

The three *gunas* are three "cosmic tendencies" or "qualities", without which manifestation would be impossible. They apply at all levels of existence. At the physical level, for example, a feather would be sattvic, a ball of lead would be tamasic, and a forest fire would be rajasic. At the level of human temperaments, a St. Francis of Assisi would be sattvic, an obtuse or evil man would be tamasic, and a man of irascible, passionate, or pugnacious tendency (whether for good or ill) would be rajasic. Every creature represents a different mix of these three qualities.

*

In Greek cosmology, the "four elements" described by Pythagoras and Empedocles are "air", "fire", "water", and "earth". Their principle or "quintessence" (*quinta essentia*) is "ether".

In Hinduism, according to the "point of view" (*darshana*) of *sânkhya* ("cosmology") (see page 69), there is a correspondence to the Greek "four elements" and their "quintessence" in the form of the "five corporeal manifestations" (*bhûtas*). These are as follows:

âkâsha	"ether"
vâyu	"air"
tejas	"fire"
ap	"water"
prithvî	"earth"

(12) The four castes

As was explained in section (1), religion originates in revelation, is handed down by tradition, and is preserved by orthodoxy. In Hinduism, the principal means whereby the revelation (both in its timeless essence and in its many outward branches) is handed down and preserved is intimately linked with the social institution known as the caste system. It is ironic that it is this, more than almost anything else, that is misunderstood and abhorred in the modern West; nothing is more vigorously anathematized by sociologists and journalists alike. Yet besides its function of preservation and transmission, the caste system is the very principle of Hindu social harmony. Caste and traditional Hindu society are virtually one and the same thing.

The four basic castes are as follows:

brahmins	"Lords Spiritual"	(priests) [sacerdotal caste]
kshatriyas	"Lords Temporal"	(kings, princes, nobles) [royal caste]
vaishyas	"third estate", "middle class"	(craftsmen, farmers, merchants)
shûdras	"laboring class"	(unskilled laborers, serfs)

The first three castes are called *dvijas* ("twice-born"), meaning that they are capable of following the spiritual life. They possess initiative, in contradistinction from the unskilled, whose essential virtue is obedience to direction from above. The *brahmins* and the *kshatriyas* constitute the nobility. The *brahmins* and the *vaishyas* are by nature peaceable and (potentially) contemplative; the *kshatriyas* and the *shûdras* are by nature active and (potentially) violent. It will be seen from the foregoing how the four Hindu castes are analogous to the four estates of Medieval Christendom. And, as any reader of the *Republic* is aware, the notion of social and functional hierarchy was well known to Plato.

Above caste are the *sannyâsins* (those who have renounced social life to become hermits) and below caste are the *chandâlas* or *pariahs* (in principle, the fruits of impure unions). The latter point is "in principle" only, and does not bear, in an individual manner, on the countless souls concerned. Saints have in fact arisen from amongst the *chandâlas*. Gandhi's name for them was *harijans* ("servants of God").

The principle of caste is social hierarchy and functional differentiation, with a view to the preservation and transmission of purity and perfection, at all levels and in all sectors. The preservation of doctrinal and ritual purity by the *brahmins* is one example; acquiring, practicing, and teaching mastership in a particular art or craft is another. At the practical and human level, the caste system strongly fosters the mutual comfort and protection characteristic of the clan or guild system.

As far as the two aristocratic castes are concerned, it is duties rather than privileges that take first place. *Noblesse oblige.* The *kshatriyas* have to be ready to face death on the battlefield, just as the *brahmins* must be willing to seek spiritual death. As for the *vaishyas*, caste (and sub-caste) facilitate and foster the discipline of craftsmanship.

The four castes correspond to four fundamental and naturally-occurring human types, characters or temperaments. This differentiation or hierarchization is a fact of nature, not nurture; of heredity, not environment. It is also perpetuated and preserved by heredity; hence the forbidding of inter-caste marriage; the latter is also a means of avoiding personal and social incompatibility. It is not so much a prohibition as a defining of something that is unlikely to happen anyway. From the traditional Hindu point of view, inter-caste marriage is a recipe for personal unhappiness and social chaos.

The descriptions of the castes given above are schematic and "ideal". They characterize in principle the four fundamental strata of society, but they do not necessarily apply with accuracy to all individuals within the various Hindu castes as they exist today.

The loss of caste, or the mixing of castes, in the West, through industrialism and democracy, has given rise to a de-natured and unhappy "proletariat", to the diminution or disappearance of craftsmanship, to shortage of labor, to distinctions based on wealth alone (the majority of the *brahmins* are poor), etc., etc. Above all, the free-for-all of the casteless (or inorganic) society is a nightmare for the weak.

Regarding the *brahmins*, here is the testimony of a French traveler and a French missionary:

"We do not think that there exists in the world an aristocratic family or even a royal family which has defended itself so pitilessly against every contagion, every misalliance, every physical or moral taint. That is why, personally speaking, we cannot conceal the fact that our contact with this splendid caste has left us truly dazzled and, from the bottom of our heart, profoundly sympathetic.... To the prestige of plastic beauty the *brahmin* visibly unites that of intelligence. Especially is he gifted for the abstract sciences, for philosophy, and above all for mathematics. A man who on this score is certainly one of the most celebrated in South India, being a member of the higher council of professors of Madras University, the Rev. Fr. Honoré, declared to us that the average level of the countless *brahmin* pupils he had taught during half a century as a teacher was far above, not only the average, but even the highest category of students in European universities."

Pierre Lhande, *L'Inde Sacré*

... causing the distinction of things for the perfection of the whole, the same Divine Wisdom is also the cause of inequality. The universe would not be perfect were there but one level of goodness.

St. Thomas Aquinas: Summa Theologica.

Some Sanscrit terms associated with caste:

dharma	=	law, norm, vocation
rita	=	universal order (from which the English word "rite" derives)
jâti (descent, birth) *varna* (qualitative nature)	=	caste
hamsa	=	primordial man, before the breakdown of humanity into castes
ativarnâshrama	=	the state of being above caste
sannyâsin	=	one who is outside caste, in that he is above it (pilgrim, hermit, monk)
chandâla *pariah*	=	one who is outside caste, in that he is below it (outcaste, untouchable)

Universal Man (Purusha)

The Brahmin was his mouth;   (Brâhmana)
from his arms was made the Ruler;   (Râjanya)
his thighs were the Industrious;   (Vaishya)
from his feet was born the Servant.   (Shûdra)

Purusha-Sûkta, Rig-Veda, X, 90.

Man's needs and aspirations are expressed in the four *purushârthas:*

artha	livelihood
kâma	sentiment, love
dharma	law, norm, vocation
moksha	salvation, deliverance

It is said that:

dharma holds *artha* and *kâma* in equilibrium;

dharma without *artha* and *kâma* leads to Heaven (*moksha*);

artha and *kama* without *dharma* lead to hell.

(13) The three spiritual ways (*mârgas*)

Mârga means a spiritual way or path. Having in mind the two sisters who offered hospitality to Christ, one speaks in Christianity of the "way of Martha" and the "way of Mary". The former is the "way of action" and the latter the "way of contemplation". Although seldom rendered explicit in Christianity, the latter "way" nevertheless comprises two modes, namely, the "way of love" and the "way of knowledge". Thus we arrive at three distinct spiritual "ways", corresponding to the three fundamental spiritual temperaments: volitive, affective, and intellective.

Metaphysically speaking, the difference between the "way of love" and the "way of knowledge" is as follows: In the "way of love", God is envisaged at the level of "Being". This has as consequence that, however sublime the mystic's "state", Lord and worshiper remain distinct. In the "way of knowledge", on the other hand, God is envisaged at the level of "Beyond-Being" or "Divine Essence". At this level it is perceived that Lord and worshiper share a common essence, and this opens up the possibility of ultimate Divine Union.

The famous formula of union *Tat tvam asi* ("thou art That") is found in the *Upanishads*. It is the foundation of the way of knowledge (*jñâna-mârga*), and signifies that man's deepest reality is one with the Supreme Principle or Divine Essence. Words such as these may arouse a suspicion of pantheism, but this is completely unjustified (see page 83). The metaphysical doctrine (of an "immanentist" nature) that Lord and worshiper share a common essence finds its counterpart in the theological dogma (of a "transcendentalist" nature) that God is man's Creator and final Judge. All the great world religions are preserved from heresy in this domain by the presence in each of them of a full recognition of both the transcendence of God and the immanence of God. Transcendentalism without immanentism leads to a kind of "deism"; immanentism without transcendentalism leads to subjectivistic delusion.

In Hinduism, the three spiritual ways are known as the three *mârgas*. They are: *karma-mârga* ("the way of works"), *bhakti-mârga* ("the way of devotion"), and *jñâna-mârga* ("the way of knowledge or gnosis"). A follower of the way of *bhakti* is known as a *bhakta* (or devotee), and a follower of the way of *jñâna* is known as a *jñânin* (or gnostic). The three *mârgas* broadly correspond to the three fundamental degrees or stations of Sufism: *makhâfa* ("Fear of God"), *mahabba* ("Love of God"), and *ma'rifa* ("Knowledge of God").

In this domain it is important to remember that "the greater contains the lesser": both the Way of Love and the Way of Knowledge necessarily contain an element of Fear, and likewise the Way of Knowledge necessarily contains within it the reality of Love. As for the Way of Love, which is composed of faith and devotion, it contains an indirect element of *jñâna* in the form of dogmatic and speculative theology. This element is in the intellectual speculation as such, not in its object, the latter (as explained on the preceding page) being limited by definition. Were this not so, it would not be a question of *bhakti*.

As for the question as to which of the paths a given aspirant will follow, it is overwhelmingly a matter of temperament and vocation: the Way chooses the individual, not the individual the Way.

The *jñânin* possesses a spiritual temperament such that, when confronted with a problem, he requires that it be solved, quite simply, according to the nature of things. The *bhakta*, on the other hand, possesses a spiritual temperament such that, when confronted with a problem, he expects to be prescribed extra prayer, fasting, penance, etc. Mystical transports are more characteristic of the *bhakta*; mental sobriety, intellection, and profound peace are more characteristic of the *jñânin*.

It is interesting to note that, historically speaking, Christian mysticism has been characterized in the main by the "way of love", whereas Hindu mysticism (like Islamic mysticism) comprises both the "way of love" and the "way of knowledge". Those who, by way of exception, have manifested the "way of knowledge" in Christianity include such great figures as Dionysius the Areopagite, Meister Eckhart and Angelus Silesius. It is precisely the writings of "gnostics" or *jñânins* such as these that have tended to cause ripples in the generally devotional or "bhaktic" climate of Christianity.

As the three fundamental spiritual temperaments are to be found throughout all mankind, the corresponding spiritual ways are present, in one shape or form, in virtually all religions.

How the three classic spiritual ways appear in the various religions is shown in the table of correspondences opposite.

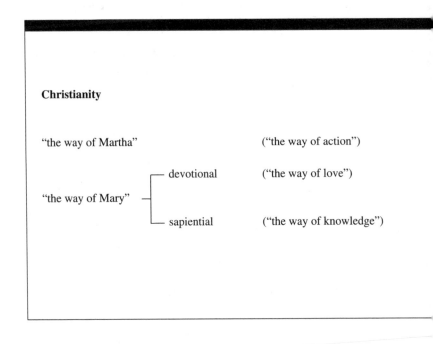

Christianity

"the way of Martha"   ("the way of action")

           devotional   ("the way of love")

"the way of Mary"

           sapiential   ("the way of knowledge")

Hinduism	Islam
karma-mârga ("the way of works")	*makhâfa* ("the fear of God")
bhakti-mârga ("the way of devotion")	*mahabba* ("the love of God")
jñâna-mârga ("the way of knowledge")	*ma'rifa* ("the knowledge of God")

There is no lustral water like unto Knowledge.

Bhagavad-Gîtâ, IV, 38.

(14) Yoga

In section (1) it was explained that religion comprises dogma and sacrament, theory and practice, doctrine and method. So far, we have spoken chiefly about the first of these two elements, namely theory or doctrine. We now turn our attention to the second element, spiritual method or practice.

Like doctrine, the spiritual method (the sacrament, the means of grace) is revealed. Initiative from the side of man is not to invent doctrine or to improvise method; the role of human initiative is to strive to understand doctrine, and to make an effort to put the corresponding "spiritual method" into effect. René Guénon referred to the latter process as "spiritual realization".

In Christianity, the practical or operative side of religion is to attend church, and there to engage in communal prayer and receive the sacraments. This may be supplemented by private prayer, often on a daily basis. Classically, the spiritual method in Christianity is "prayer and fasting"; and indeed, this dual prescription is to be found in virtually every religion.

In Hinduism, anything that pertains to the operative or "realizational" side of religion can be included under the heading of *yoga*. *Yoga* shares the same root as the Latin *iugum* and the English "yoke", and means in Sanscrit "union": the goal of *yoga* is union with the divine — at whatever level and in whatever mode. The etymology of the term inevitably evokes the words of Christ: "My yoke is easy and my burden is light (*iugum meum suave est, et onus meum leve*)."

A practitioner of *yoga* is called a *yogî* or *yogin.*

There are different forms of *yoga*, which, following an indication by Frithjof Schuon, may be classified as shown on page 57.

South Indian temple
(The Minakshi Temple, Madurai)

Umâ worshiping Shiva
(Kangra, 18th century,
Prince of Wales Museum, Bombay)

Branches of Yoga

Yoga

hatha-yoga

(psycho-physical preparation
for spiritual practice,
e.g., ascesis, breathing
techniques, hieratic postures)

raja-yoga

(the mental art of concentration;
meditation; contemplation)

laya-yoga (tantra)

(an advanced mode of *hatha-yoga* based on the positive
symbolism of the created
world; union with the
celestial archetypes of
created things; *tantra* has
been called "the fifth
veda" or "the *veda* for the
present age" [*Kali-Yuga*]).

mantra-yoga (japa-yoga)

(the repetition of a revealed
Name or Formula [*mantra*] as a
vehicle for "God-consciousness";
the systematic invocation of a
Divine Name; analogous to the
"remembrance of God" (*dhikr
Allâh*) of Sufism and the
"Jesus-Prayer" of Hesychasm)

One also encounters the terms *karma-yoga*, *bhakti-yoga*, and *jñâna-yoga*, which refer to ways of union in which the emphasis is placed respectively on meritorious works, devotion, or knowledge.

The essence of *japa-yoga* (the methodic invocation of a revealed Name of God) is succinctly summed up in the saying of Shrî Râmakrishna: "God and His Name are one." It is also elucidated by the ternary *Sat-Chit-Ânanda*, which may be translated not only as "Being-Consciousness-Bliss" and "Object-Subject-Union" (see page 20), but also as "Known-Knower-Knowledge" and "Beloved-Lover-Love", the last two expressions pertaining to *jñâna* and *bhakti* respectively. The "operative" or "spiritual" application of this ternary is even more evident in the translation "Invoked-Invoker-Invocation", which makes clear just how "God and His Name are one": in the last analysis, it is God Himself who invokes, God Himself who is invoked, and God Himself who is the invocation. That this divine Act should pass through man is precisely the mystery and sacrament of union.

Some Sanscrit terms relating to spiritual realization

moksha	=	salvation, deliverance, liberation, enlightenment
jîvan-mukta	=	one who achieves *moksha* in this life
videha-mukta	=	one who achieves *moksha* on death
samâdhi	=	mystical rapture, ecstasy

(15) The Hindu Scriptures*

Hinduism, the *Sanâtana Dharma* ("Perennial Law" or "Primordial Norm"), is considered to have existed from all eternity. Its scriptures were revealed (the earliest of them a millennium or more B.C.) through the *rishis* or "seers", who received them by "visual intuition" (*drishti*) from God.

In the Hindu scriptures there are two levels or degrees of inspiration — primary and secondary — known respectively as *shruti* and *smriti. Shruti* ("aural intuition") refers to those books that act as vehicle for the transmission of the primordial tradition, while *smriti* ("remembrance") refers to those books that continue the revelation of the primordial tradition.

Shruti includes the *Vedas*, the *Samhitâs*, the *Brâhmanas*, the *Âranyakas*, and the *Upanishads.*

Smriti includes the *Upavedas* ("branches of the *Vedas*"), the *Vedângas* ("limbs of the *Vedas*"), the *Sûtras* ("guides"), the *Shâstras* ("textbooks"), the *Purânas* ("old stories"), and the *Râmâyana* and the *Mahâbhârata* (the two great Hindu epics). The last-mentioned incorporates the *Bhagavad-Gîtâ* ("the Song of the Lord"), which, paradoxically, is a revelation of primary rank (*shruti*), and is perhaps the most renowned of all the Hindu scriptures.

The writings of the great classical "doctors" of Hinduism-Patañjali, Shankara, Râmânuja, and Madhva (see page 85) — also pertain to *smriti.*

---

*See "Introduction to the Hindu Scriptures" by V. Raghavan in *The Religion of the Hindus* edited by Kenneth Morgan (Ronald Press Co, N.Y., 1953) and *Sacred Writings* by Günter Lanczkowski (Collins, London;Harper & Row, New York; 1956).

The Vedas

The most ancient and primordial of all the revealed books of Hinduism are the *Vedas*, which are four in number. (*Veda* = "knowledge".) Corresponding to the four *Vedas* are the four *Upavedas*, which contain knowledge of a secondary or applied nature. Thus:

Rig-Veda	(hymns)	*Âyur-Veda*	(medicine)
Yajur-Veda	(sacrificial formulas)	*Dhanur-Veda*	(military science)
Sâma-Veda	(chants and tunes)	*Gandharva-Veda*	(music)
Atharva-Veda	(magic texts)	*Sthâpatya-Veda*	(mechanics and architecture)

The Upanishads

The *Upanishads* are also referred to as the *Vedânta* ("the end of the *Vedas*"). They contain what might be called the metaphysical or esoteric doctrine of the *Vedas*. The principal *Upanishads* are *Brihadâranyaka, Taittiriya, Mundaka, Mândûkya, Katha, Chhândogya, Shvetâshvatara*, and *Îsha*.

श्रीदक्षिणामूर्तयेनमः

॥ श्रीदक्षिणामूर्तिस्तोत्रम् ॥

मौनव्याख्याप्रकटितपरब्रह्मतत्त्वं युवानं वर्षिष्ठान्तेवसदृषिगणैर्गवृतं ब्रह्मनिष्ठैः।
आचार्येन्द्रं करकलितचिन्मुद्रमानन्दमूर्ति स्वात्मारामं मुदितवदनं दक्षिणामूर्तिमीडे ॥१॥

चित्रं वटतरोर्मूले वृद्धशिष्या गुरुर्युवा ।
गुरोस्तु मौनं व्याख्यानं शिष्यास्तु छिन्नसंशयाः॥१०॥

ओं नमः प्रणवार्थाय शुद्धज्ञानैकमूर्तये ।
निर्मलाय प्रशान्ताय दक्षिणामूर्तये नमः॥५॥

निधये सर्वविद्यानां भिषजे भवरोगिणाम्।
गुरवे सर्वलोकानां दक्षिणामूर्तये नमः॥६॥

वटविटपिसमीपे भूमिभागे निषण्णं सकलमुनिजनानां ज्ञानदातारमारात्।
त्रिभुवनगुरुमीशं दक्षिणामूर्तिदेवं जननमरणदुःखच्छेददक्षं नमामि॥१०॥

Hymn to Dakshinâmûrti
Sanscrit text in *devanâgarî* script
(calligraphy by Shrî Keshavram Iengar)

The Vedângas

"*Vedânga* means 'limb of the *Veda*', and this name is applied to certain auxiliary sciences of the *Veda* which are compared to the bodily limbs by means of which a being acts outwardly; the fundamental treatises relating to these sciences form part of *smriti*, in which they occupy the first place by reason of their direct relationship with the *Veda*."* The *vedângas* are six in number, as follows:

		part of body to which symbolically related
shikshâ	articulation, euphony, symbolism of letters	nose (breath)
chhandas	prosody, laws of verse	feet
vyâkarana	grammar	mouth
nirukta	etymology, exegesis	ears
jyotisha	astronomy and astrology	eyes
kalpa	the science of rites	hands

---

*René Guénon: *Introduction to the Study of the Hindu Doctrines* (Luzac, London, 1945)

The Shâstras

The *Dharma Shâstras* ("legal textbooks") include the *Mânava-Dharma-Shâstra* (the "Laws of Manu"), which codifies all the laws relating to Hindu life and society, and the *Bharata-Nâtya-Shâstra* (revealed by Shiva to the sage Bharata), which codifies the canons for the sacred arts of sculpture, dance, music, and drama.

The Purânas

The eighteen *Purânas* are a voluminous source of Hindu doctrine and mythology. For an extract from the *Vishnu-Purâna*, see pages 74-76.

The Râmâyana and the Mahâbhârata

See section (16) on page 65: "The Hindu Epics".

I vouchsafe security against all creatures to him who comes to Me even once and seeks protection from Me, saying: "I am Thine." This is My vow.

Râmâyana, VI, 18, 33.

(16) The Hindu Epics

Reference was made on page 9 to the similarities between the Hindu religion and that of Greece and Rome. Amongst other things, it was pointed out that, in both cases, much of the mythology (the natural "language" of the exoteric religion) finds expression in epic poems. In the case of Greece, there are the two epic poems of Homer: the *Iliad*, which tells the story of the Trojan war, and the *Odyssey*, which tells the story of the wanderings, and final return home, of the hero of that war, Odysseus or Ulysses. In the case of Rome, there is Virgil's Latin epic, the *Aeneid*, which recounts the adventurous journey of Aeneas (one of the defenders of Troy) to Latium, preceding the foundation of Rome.

Such great and providential epics, full of inexhaustible riches, are typical of, and of virtually central importance in, the religions that are known as the Aryan mythologies. They are an inspired source of knowledge and wisdom, and of spiritual and moral education. They poetically enshrine the religious myths, and give the semi-legendary history of the respective peoples a cosmic setting. This consecration of history permits it to become an integral and even central element in the religious form concerned.

Christianity, on the other hand, derives its form and its expression from Christ and the Gospels. Nevertheless, there is in Christianity one epic poem which at least in some respects is comparable to those of Greece and Rome: this is the *Divine Comedy* of

Dante. It is because of the comparable grandeur of this poem — an inspired poetic expression of Christian doctrine — that Dante was able to regard himself as a successor to Homer and Virgil.

In Hinduism, the two great epic poems, in the Sanscrit language, are the *Râmâyana* (attributed to Vâlmîki) and the *Mahâbhârata* (attributed to Krishna Dvaipâyana Vyâsa). The story of Râma, whose *Shakti*, or Consort, is Sîtâ, is related in the *Râmâyana*. The story of Krishna, whose Consort is Râdhâ, is related in the *Mahâbhârata*.

As already mentioned, the two great epics of Hinduism pertain to the secondary degree of revelation known as *smriti*. Paradoxically, however, the *Mahâbhârata* contains within it the *Bhagavad-Gîtâ* ("the Lord's Song"), which is a revelation of primary rank, and is perhaps the most renowned of all the scriptures of Hinduism.

For a comment by Frithjof Schuon on the practical spiritual significance for Hindus of these two epics, see page 109.

Râma
(Bronze statue, Madras, 15th century,
Victoria and Albert Museum, London)

Rise, awake! Having obtained thy boons, understand them!
The sharp edge of a razor is difficult to pass over;
thus, say the wise, the way to Salvation is hard.

Katha Upanishad, I, 3, 14.

(17) The six points of view (*darshanas*)

In the rich treasury of Hindu doctrine, there are six traditional areas of study known as the six *darshanas* ("points of view"). *Darshana* comes from the root *drish* which means "to see".

The six *darshanas*, grouped in three pairs and in traditional order, are as follows:

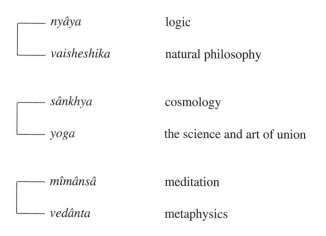

nyâya	logic
vaisheshika	natural philosophy
sânkhya	cosmology
yoga	the science and art of union
mîmânsâ	meditation
vedânta	metaphysics

A reference to Hindu cosmology (*sânkhya*) is made on pages 41-42, *yoga* is dealt with on pages 55-58, and metaphysics (*vedânta*) on pages 15-20 and 37-40.

The term *darshana* (*darshan* in Hindi) is also used to refer to the blessing that may be obtained from the beholding or contemplating of a saint (see page 89).

Creatures are made dear, not so that you may love creatures, but so that you may love God.

Brihadâranyaka Upanishad, II, 4, 5.

(18) Vishnuism and Shivaism

In metaphysics, as in mysticism, one encounters the notions of a "Personal" God and an "Impersonal" (or "Supra-Personal") God. This fundamental metaphysical distinction was already referred to on page 15, where it was pointed out that the "Personal" God corresponds to Being, and the "Impersonal" (or "Supra-Personal") God to Beyond-Being or the Divine Essence.

Likewise, on page 49, the difference between the "way of love" and the "way of knowledge" was characterized in terms of the different ways in which God is envisaged. In the "way of love", God is envisaged at the level of "Being" (which has as consequence that Lord and worshiper always remain distinct); in the "way of knowledge", on the other hand, God is envisaged at the level of "Beyond-Being" or "Divine Essence" (and here it is perceived that Lord and worshiper share a common essence, thus opening up the possibility of ultimate Divine Union). The "way of love" is thus a "bhaktic" way centered on the Personal God, whereas the "way of knowledge" is a "jñânic" way that has in view the Supra-Personal God or the Divine Essence.

These two degrees of envisaging Ultimate Reality are to be found in Hinduism, and are represented by the two approaches to God known as Vishnuism and Shivaism. It is evident that the two approaches concerned take their names respectively from the second and third Persons of the *Trimûrti* (page 23), namely, *Vishnu* (the Preserver) and *Shiva* (the Destroyer or Transformer). In broad terms, it might be said that the followers of Vishnuism (*Vaishnavas*) worship *Îshvara*, the Personal God, and follow a bhaktic way, while the followers of Shivaism (*Shaivas*) are centered on *Brahman*, the Divine Essence, and follow a jñanic way.

The great *Shaiva* exponent of *jñâna-mârga* (the way of knowledge) was Shrî Shankarâchârya, who lived in the 9th century, and the great *Vaishnava* exponent of *bhakti-mârga* (the way of love) was Shrî Râmânuja, who lived in the 11th century.

At the outward level, it is obvious that the formulations of the bhaktic viewpoint may conflict with the deeper jñânic vision. Essentially, however, there is no contradiction, for the precise reason that the two viewpoints are situated at different levels. Here, as elsewhere, it can be said that "the greater contains the lesser". *Bhakti* (devotion or love), in the appropriate mode, is contained within *jñâna* (knowledge).

There is no right superior to that of truth.

Maxim of the Maharajas of Benares.

(19) The four ages (*yugas*)

Hinduism possesses an elaborate theory of cosmic cycles.
The simplest presentation of this, derived from the *Mânava-Dharma-Shâstra*, may be expressed as follows:

4 *Yugas*	=	1 *Mahâyuga*
71 *Mahâyugas*	=	1 *Manvantara*
14 *Manvantaras*	=	1 *Kalpa* ("Day of *Brahmâ*")
360 (x 2) *Kalpas*	=	1 *Para* ("Year of *Brahmâ*")
994 ("1000") *Mahâyugas*	=	1 *Kalpa*

Each *Mahâyuga* ("eon"), including our own, is thus made up of four *Yugas* ("ages"). These are as follows:

			relative duration in the following proportion
(1)	*Krita-Yuga (Satya-Yuga)*	Golden Age	4
(2)	*Treta-Yuga*	Silver Age	3
(3)	*Dvapara-Yuga*	Bronze Age	2
(4)	*Kali-Yuga* ("Dark Age")	Iron Age	1
			10

According to the Hindu chronology for the present *Mahâyuga* or eon, we have already entered the last phase of the *Kali-Yuga* or "Dark Age". One of the Hindu scriptures, the *Vishnu-Purâna* (codified in approximately the 3rd century A.D.), contains a prophetic description of the conditions which will characterize this latter part of the Dark Age:

"Riches and piety will diminish daily, until the world will be completely corrupted. In those days it will be wealth that confers distinction, passion will be the sole reason for union between the sexes, lies will be the only method for success in business, and women will be the objects merely of sensual gratification. The earth will be valued only for its mineral treasures, dishonesty will be the universal means of subsistence, a simple ablution will be regarded as sufficient purification...

"The observance of castes, laws, and institutions will no longer be in force in the Dark Age, and the ceremonies prescribed by the *Vedas* will be neglected. Women will obey only their whims and will be infatuated with pleasure... Men of all kinds will presumptuously regard themselves as the equals of *brahmins**... The *vaishyas* will abandon agriculture and commerce and will earn their living by servitude or by the exercise of mechanical professions... The path of the *Vedas* having been abandoned, and man having been led astray from orthodoxy, iniquity will prevail and the length of human life will diminish in consequence... Then men will cease worshiping Vishnu, the Lord of sacrifice, Creator and Lord of all things, and they will say: 'Of what authority are the *Vedas*? Who are the Gods and the *brahmins*? What use is purification with water?...'

---

*For an explanation of the Hindu castes, see section (12) on page 43.

The dominant caste will be that of *shûdras*... Men, deprived of reason and subject to every infirmity of body and mind, will daily commit sins: everything which is impure, vicious, and calculated to afflict the human race will make its appearance in the Dark Age."

(20) The four stages in life (*âshramas*)

Ideally speaking, Hinduism envisages man's earthly existence as comprising four successive stages or *âshramas* ("periods of spiritual effort"). These are as follows:

(1) *brahmacharya* = youth, celibacy, study of the sacred science and of one's calling

(2) *gârhasthya* = state of married life or householder

(3) *vanaprastha* = relative renunciation of the world and society

(4) *sannyâsa* = total renunciation

The term *âshrama* (or *âshram*) can also mean "place of spiritual effort", and the hermitages or retreats of holy men are generally referred to as *âshrams*.

God, the Maker of all things, dwells in the heart of man. He is perceived by the heart, the soul, and the mind. Those who know Him transcend death.

Shvetâshvatara Upanishad, IV, 17.

(21) Transmigration

As we have seen, there is in Hinduism an elaborate theory of cosmic cycles. Linked with this is the doctrine of transmigration — or multiple births and re-births — frequently, but misleadingly, referred to as "reincarnation".

In the modern West, the notion of "reincarnation" has been adopted by many pseudo-esoterists, who, in the grossest manner imaginable, profess to believe in it literally, envisaging a series of human re-births in this world. It is true that a literal attitude towards transmigration is also to be found among the Hindu masses, and indeed such a belief derives from a literal interpretation of the Hindu scriptures. However, the most simple Hindu peasant, even if he looks on transmigration literally, has an infinitely more subtle intuition of the moral and spiritual implications of this doctrine than the grotesque pseudo-esoterists of the West. In India, a literalist attitude towards transmigration is not only harmless, but may even be beneficial. The gross "reincarnationism" of renegade Christian pseudo-esoterists, on the other hand, is immensely harmful and destructive.

For a Hindu, a literal belief in transmigration is like a Christian believing that hell is a fiery furnace down below. It may not be strictly true — and yet it is not false either, because the image is one which is adequate to the truth in question and, being so, has had a salutary moral and spiritual effect for countless generations (including the much-despised "fundamentalists" of today). Let it be said in passing that, compared with the average "modern" man, a "fundamentalist" is like a Plato.[1]

---

[1] We refer here only to authentic fundamentalists, of whatever denomination or religion, not to hypocrites or criminals wrongly categorized as such.

The point is that elements plucked from one religious imagery (though in themselves "figures of truth") are often not transplantable to another; above all, they cannot be transplanted, without grave results, from a traditional world into the chaotic modern world, where there is minimal religious instruction and minimal religious sensibility.

The Hindu doctrine of transmigration refers to the posthumous journeying of the unsanctified soul through an indefinite series of "peripheral" or "central" (but, quite emphatically, nonterrestrial) states[2]. According to the Hindus, the "central" state — i.e. analogous to the human state in the terrestrial world — is "difficult to obtain", and consequently man must not squander the precious opportunity to use it for the purpose for which it is intended. The Hindus graphically indicate what this purpose is by saying that it is the *dharma* of water to flow, of fire to burn, of fish to swim, of birds to fly, and of man to achieve salvation.[3]

In some respects, transmigration may be regarded as the mythological analogue of the theological doctrine of purgatory — with the important difference, however, that a soul in purgatory has definitively retained its "central" state and is assured of eventual paradise, whereas the final fate of a soul in transmigration may still be hell. At this point the Aryan and Semitic eschatologies do not entirely coincide.[4]

---

[2] René Guénon often emphasized that "no being of any kind can pass through the same state twice".

[3] *Dharma* = "inner law" or "vocation".

[4] See: *Survey of Metaphysics and Esoterism* by Frithjof Schuon, chapter entitled "Universal Eschatology" (World Wisdom Books, Bloomington. Indiana, 1982).

A revealing discrepancy between the Hindu theory of a succession of births and deaths (for the unsanctified or unsaved soul) and the fantastical reincarnationism of Western cults is that the Hindu strives at all costs to avoid re-birth, which would be "peripheral" and sorrowful, and in another world, whereas the pseudo-esoterist imprudently (but illusorily) hankers after a further life or lives, which he imagines will be "central" and happy, and in this world! The pseudo-esoterist may be pushed towards a vain belief in reincarnationism because — rightly — he has an intuition that he is deserving of hell (and, in any case, his decisively erroneous views block any move in the direction of Heaven). The Hindu seeks to escape from the "round of existence"; the impious heretic longs to remain within it. For the orthodox Hindu there could be no clearer proof of his perversity!

Directly linked with transmigration is the doctrine of *karma* (the effect of past actions): "as a man sows, so shall he reap".

He who knoweth Him, knoweth himself,
and is not afraid to die.

Atharva Veda, X, 8, 44.

(22) The question of "pantheism"

Very often the term "pantheism" is applied to Oriental doctrines, especially the metaphysical and/or mystical doctrines of Vedânta, Taoism, and Sufism. The immediate and formal answer to this is that no traditional doctrine is pantheistic, since the vague, superficial, and contradictory notion of pantheism (a material or substantial identity between two different levels of reality) is a purely modern phenomenon.

What rescues all traditional doctrine from the charge of pantheism is, in a word, transcendence: God is transcendent, and there is no material, formal, or substantial identity between creation and the Creator. This applies also in the case of Hindu and Greek "emanationism", in which the Principle remains wholly transcendent of any of its manifestations.

Of course all metaphysical or mystical doctrines (be they Oriental, Greek, or Christian) are doctrines of union. (There are different degrees of union — ontological or supra-ontological — as has already been mentioned.) Christ said: "I and the Father are one," and the Christian way is essentially to unite oneself with Christ. In Hinduism, it is said that "all things are Âtmâ". This means (and it is in accordance with the doctrine of Plato) that all things have their principle on a level of reality *above* the one on which they "exist", and that the Principle of principles is Âtmâ. There is indeed "essential" identity, but there is "substantial" discontinuity.

In Hinduism it is also said: "The world is false, *Brahma* is true", while in Christianity it is said: "Heaven and earth shall pass away, but My words will not pass away." To allude to the ephemerality of all created things (something that has been known from time immemorial) is not pantheism; it is what all religions regard as true doctrine.

It is true that there are mystical and scriptural expressions (both Christian and Oriental) which use figures of material continuity, for example, when it is said that all creatures are vessels made from the same Clay, or that all rivers return to the one Ocean; or again, when Christ says: "I am the vine, ye are the branches." However, the symbolic nature of such utterances is perfectly clear, and in any case the orthodox commentaries within each tradition ensure that the element of transcendence is not overlooked.

The idea of a formal or substantial identity between two different levels of reality (or the obtuseness of taking such an idea literally) devolves on European philosophers and poets of recent centuries. The idea is totally devoid of profundity and does not in fact have much meaning; it is foreign to any traditional perspective.

(23) Classical sages and saints

In the history of Christianity, one speaks of the "doctors of the Church". If such an expression were permissible in the case of Hinduism, the list of "doctors" would be long, and would surely include Manu (codifier of the *Mânava-Dharma-Shâstra* or the "Laws of Manu"), Bharatamuni (codifier of the *Bharata-Nâtya-Shâstra*), Vâlmîki (compiler of the *Râmâyana*), and Krishna Dvaipâyana Vyâsa (compiler of the *Mahâbhârata*), all mentioned elsewhere in these pages. From amongst many other eminent "doctors", we now single out the following:

Patañjali (around 100 B.C. — 100 A.D)

Patañjali was the author of the *Yoga-Sûtras*, which expound the methods of *râja-yoga*, for which *hatha-yoga* is a preparation.

Shankara (c. 788-820 A.D.)

Shankara was the classic exponent of "non-dualism" (*advaita*) and undoubtedly the greatest teacher ever of the "way of knowledge" (*jñâna-mârga*) or pure and unconditional metaphysics. He is often referred to as Shrî Shankarâchârya. *Shrî*, the literal Sanscrit meaning of which is "radiance" or "glory", is an honorific, sometimes translated as "Lord"; *âchârya* means "teacher". The term "non-dualism" is, so to speak, a double negative, and has parallels in the other Vedantic phrase "the One without a second" and in the Islamic expression "He who has no associate" (*lâ sharîka la-Hu*).

Shankara is the author of detailed commentaries on the *Upanishads*, the *Bhagavad-Gîtâ*, and other scriptures. Amongst his best-known works are *Âtmâ-Bodha* ("Knowledge of the Self") and *Viveka-chûda-mâni* ("The Crest Jewel of Discrimination").

Râmânuja (1050-1137)

Shrî Râmânuja was the exponent of "differentiated non-dualism" (*vishishtâdvaita*), and his spiritual attitude was that of *bhakti-mârga*. Outwardly, his formulations may conflict with those of the advaitic and jñânic vision of Shankara, but there is no essential contradiction, for the precise reason that the two view-points are situated at different levels. (See the first two paragraphs on page 49.) Here, as elsewhere, it can be said that "the greater contains the lesser": *bhakti* (devotion), in the apopropriate mode, is contained within *jñâna* (knowledge).

Madhva (1199-1278)

Shrî Madhva taught "dualism" (*savisheshâdvaita*). He wrote commentaries on the *Upanishads* and the *Bhagavad-Gîtâ*.

Chaitanya (1486-1534)

Shrî Chaitanya was a *vaishnava* who taught that the invocation of the Name of God (*japa*) was the most effective spiritual method in the *Kali-Yuga* (Dark Age).

(24) Jagadgurus and Shankarâchâryas

We spoke on page 85 of the original Shrî Shankarâchârya (*Adi-Shankarâchârya*), the inspired exponent of metaphysical doctrine, who flourished in the 9th century A.D. Shankara's function, as *jñâna-yogin* and master of *advaita-vâda* ("the way of non-duality"), was to formulate and expound the truth, to give expression to ultimate reality.

There is an authentic line of spiritual descent from the original Shankarâchârya down to the present day. It is refracted into five traditional seats (*pîthas*), traditions (*âmnâyas*), or establishments (*maths*), all of them regular and valid. All five of the holders of these offices bear the title of *Shankarâchârya* and these Shankarâchârya have their official seats respectively at Badrinath (in the north), Puri (in the east), Dvarkâ (in the west), Kanchipuram (in the south), and Shringeri (also in the south). Each Shankarâchârya also has the title of *Jagadguru* or "universal teacher" (*jagad* literally signifying "world").

There are many paths that lead to God. In India, as elsewhere, the one that is most widespread is that of "devotion" (*bhakti*). However, for their respective regions of India, these spiritual descendents of the original *Shankarâchârya* traditionally and symbolically represent the uncolored light of knowledge or gnosis (*jñâna*).

Each Shankarâchârya has, so to speak, a circuit: that is to say, he travels publicly and ceremonially, accompanied by his suite. The suite may include elephants, camels, cows, and musicians. For the collectivity in general, he exercises his function in a manner that the Buddhists might describe as an "activity of presence": he is a blessing, not merely for what he teaches, but above all for what he (or his office) *is*. In this respect at least, his role is analogous to, and has the importance of, that of a temporal monarch.

*
* *

Five *Pîthas* of Shankarâchârya   (Five Shankara *Maths*)

N	-	Badrinath	(*Jyotirmath*)
E	-	Puri	(*Govardhanamath*)
W	-	Dvarkâ	(*Kâlikâmath*)
S	-	Shringeri	(*Sharadâmath*)
S	-	Kâñci	(*Kâmikôtimath*)

Krishna and Râdhâ
(Kangra, 18th century, Benares Hindu University)

Pârvati
(Bronze statue, Madras, 10th-12th century

(25) Modern sages and saints

The sages and saints teach the truth and the way of salvation. Hindus consider it important to frequent sages and saints, in order to learn by precept and example, and to obtain a blessing. Such frequentation is called *sat-sanga*, which literally means "association with truth (or reality)".

In some cases it may be a question of a spiritual relationship between a spiritual master (*guru*) and a disciple (*shishya*).*

It is considered that the mere beholding of a saint, or even of his picture, confers a significant blessing. This is known as "receiving the *darshan* of a saint".

Here follows an album of modern sages and saints:

---

*It should perhaps be mentioned here that, in the last decade or two, inauthentic Hindu *gurus* have become ten-a-penny in the west.

Shrî Râmakrishna Paramahansa (1836-1886)

Shrî Râmakrishna was born in a Bengali village. As a young man, he went to Calcutta, but refused to acquire a modern secular education. At the age of 30, he became a priest in the temple at Dakshineshwar, where he remained for most of his life. He is reputed to have obtained the vision of God by following the paths laid down in the Scriptures. He had direct experience of Christianity and Islam, and was the first spiritual authority in modern times explicitly to teach the transcendent unity of all the revealed and orthodox religions. His instruction on the sacramental nature of invocatory prayer is summed up in his saying: "God and His Name are one." His teachings are enshrined in *The Gospel of Shri Ramakrishna*, a comprehensive record by Mahendranath Gupta of his talks, over many years, with his disciples and intimates.

Swami Bhaskarânanda (19th century)

Shrî Swami Bhaskarânanda was born around 1828 and flourished in Benares. The method of spiritual realization which he taught was the invocation of the Name of God (*japa*). His picture opposite calls for some comments. In Hinduism, as in other religions, sacred nudity is based on the correspondence between what is most outward and what is most inward. "Extremes meet." It is said that sacred nudity favors the irradiation of spiritual influences; and also that feminine nudity in particular manifests Lakshmî and thus has a beneficial effect on the surroundings. An example of this is the great Kashmiri saint Lallâ Yogîshvarî who, having realized God in her heart, declared: "It is for this that, naked, I dance." In Christianity, St. Gregory Palamas wrote: "In spiritual men, the uncreated grace of the Spirit, transmitted to the body through the soul, also gives knowledge of godly things to the body. God, transcending all things, consents to become participatory and invisibly visible."

Shrî Râmana Mahârshi (1879-1950)

Shrî Râmana Mahârshi was born in the outskirts of Madurai in Tamilnad. At the age of 17 years, through a spontaneous act of "Self-enquiry", he attained to the realization of God. He left home and set out as a *sâdhu* (pilgrim or hermit) for the town of Tiruvannamalai (120 miles south-west of Madras), where he spent the rest of his life. He lived in a cave on the adjacent sacred mountain of Arunachala. He was already known as *Mahârshi* ("great sage"), and disciples immediately gathered around him, addressing him in the third person as *Bhagavân*, a divine name. After some twenty years, Shrî Râmana Mahârshi came down from Arunachala to Tiruvannamalai (site of a magnificent temple) where he lived for the rest of his life. His simple abode became a world-famous *âshram* (hermitage), visited by countless people from many countries who sought his counsel. Shrî Râmana Mahârshi taught undiluted *jñâna* (knowledge of God), while emphasizing that *karma* (meritorious works) and *bhakti* (devotion or love) were necessarily contained within *jñâna*. To this day devotees perform a circumambulatory rite (*pradakshina*) around the holy mountain where he dwelt.

The Jagadguru of Kanchipuram (born 1894)

The full designation of the Jagadguru of Kanchipuram is: His Holiness the Jagadguru Shrî Chandrasekharendra Sarasvati, the 68th Shankarâchârya Svâmigal of Kâñcî Kâmakôti Pîtha. He was born in 1894, and assumed his function in 1907. At the time of writing (1991) he is still alive, at the age of 97 years. His successor, Shri Jayendra Sarasvati, known as the junior Svâmigal, was appointed many years ago, and now fills the role of head of the Kâmakoti Math (Mathâdhipati). Given the ages of these personages, a succesor to the junior Svâmigal now also exists, and there are thus at present three generations of Shankarâchâryas at Kanchipuram. See also pages 87-88.

Swami Ramdas (1884-1963)

Swami Ramdas was pre-eminently a *japa-yogin*, a votary of the Divine Name. It was in 1922 that he left his home in Mangalore in south-west India to become a wandering pilgrim (*sâdhu*) dedicated exclusively to the recitation of the Supreme Name and, for the rest of his long life, he totally identified himself with this spiritual way. He emphasized the need for complete trust in God, and taught that the unceasing invocation of the revealed Name of God was a sanctifying sacrament, and the surest and most direct way to salvation. While still at school, Swami Ramdas had joyously assimilated the works of Shakespeare, and he had a masterly command of English. His writings are a vivid instruction in the essentials of the spiritual life. His earliest and most renowned work is *In Quest of God.*

Mâ Ânanda Mâyî (1896-1982)

Mâ Ânanda Mâyî was born in North India. She was renowned as a lover of God who radiated holy joy, but at the same time was an implacable spiritual guide. People came from all over the world to seek her counsel and receive her *darshan*. She taught the two-fold way of Love and Knowledge (*bhakti* and *jñâna*).

Whoso, at the hour of death, leaves his body remembering Me, will be united with Me thereafter.

Bhagavad-Gîtâ, VIII, 5.

(26) Holy Cities, Holy Rivers, Pilgrimage Points

Seven Holy Cities

to whom sacred

Ayodhya	Vishnu (Râma)
Mathura	Vishnu (Krishna)
Haridwar (Gaya, Maya)	Shiva
Kâśî (Vârânasî, Banâras)	Shiva (Vishvanâtha)
Kâñchî (Conjeevaram)	Shiva and Vishnu
Ujjain (Avanthika)	Shiva (Mahâkâleshvara)
Dvarkâ	Vishnu (Krishna)

Seven Holy Rivers

Ganga, Yamuna, Godavari, Sarasvatî, Narmada, Sindhu, Kaveri

*

* *

Four Pilgrimage Points

N - Badrinath

S - Rameshwaram

E - Puri

W - Dvarkâ

I am the seed of all creatures; no creature, animate or inanimate, can exist without Me.

Bhagavad-Gîtâ, X, 39.

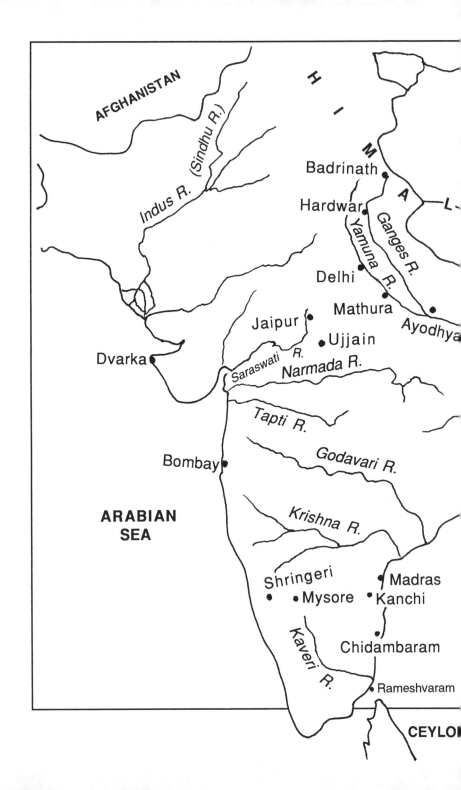

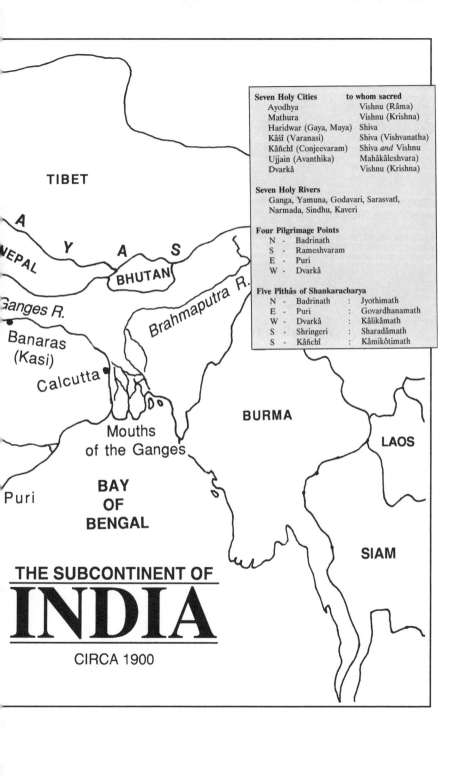

TIBET

Seven Holy Cities   **to whom sacred**
Ayodhya   Vishnu (Râma)
Mathura   Vishnu (Krishna)
Haridwar (Gaya, Maya)   Shiva
Kâsî (Varanasi)   Shiva (Vishvanatha)
Kâñchî (Conjeevaram)   Shiva *and* Vishnu
Ujjain (Avanthika)   Mahâkâleshvara)
Dvarkâ   Vishnu (Krishna)

Seven Holy Rivers
Ganga, Yamuna, Godavari, Sarasvatî,
Narmada, Sindhu, Kaveri

Four Pilgrimage Points
N - Badrinath
S - Rameshvaram
E - Puri
W - Dvarkâ

Five Pîthâs of Shankaracharya
N - Badrinath : Jyothimath
E - Puri : Govardhanamath
W - Dvarkâ : Kâlikâmath
S - Shringeri : Sharadâmath
S - Kâñchî : Kâmikôtimath

A
Y   A   S
NEPAL
BHUTAN
Ganges R.
Brahmaputra R.
Banaras
(Kasi)
Calcutta
Mouths
of the Ganges
BURMA
LAOS
Puri
BAY
OF
BENGAL
SIAM

THE SUBCONTINENT OF
INDIA
CIRCA 1900

Behold the universe in the glory of God and all that lives and moves on earth. Leaving the transient, find joy in the Eternal.

He who knows both the transcendent and the immanent, with the immanent overcomes death and with the transcendent reaches immortality.

Îshâ Upanishad, 1, 14.

(27) Two evocations of Hindu piety

Hindu Mythology as the Vehicle of Salvation

"The Hindu who invokes Shrî Râma abandons his own
existence for that of his Lord: it is as if he slept and Râma watched
and acted for him; he sleeps in Shrî Râma, in the divine form of
the Invoked, while the latter takes on all the burdens of the devotee's life and finally brings him back to this divine and immutable
form itself. The doctrine of Râma is contained in the Hindu epic,
the *Râmâyana*: the myth retraces the fate of the soul (represented
by Sîtâ) which is ravished by passion and ignorance (Râvana) and
exiled in matter, at the confines of the cosmos (Lankâ). Every soul
dedicated to Shrî Râma is identified with Sîtâ, the heroine carried
off and finally delivered.

"Râdhâ, the eternal spouse of Krishna, lends herself to the
same symbolism. The very name Krishna evokes the wisdom hid-
den in the *Mahâbhârata* (the other great Hindu epic) and expound-
ed in the *Bhagavad-Gîtâ*, which is its synthesis and flower."

Frithjof Schuon,
Stations of Wisdom, chapter 5, "Modes of Prayer".

Bathing in the Ganges

"For the Hindus, the water of life finds embodiment in the Ganges which, from its source in the Himalayas, the mountains of the Gods, irrigates the largest and most populous plains of India. Its water is held to be pure from beginning to end, and in fact it is preserved from all pollution by the fine sand which it drags along with it. Whoever, with repentant mind, bathes in the Ganges, is freed from all his sins: inner purification here finds its symbolic support in the outward purification that comes from the water of the sacred river. It is as if the purifying water came from Heaven, for its origin in the eternal ice of the roof of the world is like a symbol of the heavenly origin of divine grace which, as 'living water', springs from timeless and immutable Peace. Here, as in the similar rites of other religions and peoples, the correspondence of water and soul helps the latter to purify itself or, more exactly, to find anew its own — originally pure — essence. In this process, the symbol prepares the way for grace."

Titus Burckhardt,
Mirror of the Intellect, chapter 11, "The Symbolism of Water".

(28) Two descriptions of Hindu art

"Hindu art has in it something of the heavy motion of the sea and something of the exuberance of the virgin forest; it is sumptuous, sensual, and rhythmical; intimately linked with dancing, it seems to proceed from the cosmic dance of the Gods. In certain respects, the Tamil taste is heavier and more static than that of the Aryan Hindus of the north.

"When the arts are enumerated, the art of dress is too often forgotten.... The Hindu genius, which in a certain sense divinizes the 'wife-mother', has created a feminine dress unsurpassable in its beauty, dignity, and femininity."

Frithjof Schuon,
Spiritual Perspectives, pages 38-39.

*
* *

"In its exaltation of feminine beauty, Hindu art far surpasses Greek art, whose spiritual ideal, progressively reduced to a purely human ideal, is cosmos as opposed to the indefinity of chaos, and therefore the beauty of the male body, with its clearly articulated proportions; the supple and undivided beauty of the female body, its richness both simple and complex, like that of the sea, is absent from Greek art, at least on the intellectual level. Hellenism remains closed to the affirmation of the Infinite, which it confuses with the indefinite; lacking the conception of the transcendent Infinite, it likewise fails to perceive it at the 'prakritic' level, in other words, as the inexhaustible ocean of forms. It is not until the period of its decadence that Greek art becomes open to the 'irrational' beauty of the feminine body, but this removes it from its own *ethos*. In Hindu art, on the other hand, the feminine body appears as a spontaneous and innocent manifestation of universal rhythm, like a wave of the primordial ocean or a flower from the tree of the world.

"Something of this innocent beauty also surrounds the images of sexual union (*maithuna*) which adorn Hindu temples.

In their deepest meaning, they express the state of spiritual union, the fusion of subject and object, of inward and outward, in mystical rapture (*samâdhi*). They also symbolize the complementarism of the cosmic poles, active and passive, thus effacing the passional aspect of these images in a universal vision.

"In this way Hindu sculpture, effortlessly and without loss of spiritual unity, assimilates means which, in other hands, would lead to naturalism. It transmutes even sensuality, by saturating it with a spiritual awareness that is expressed in the plastic tension of the surfaces; like those of a bell, they seem to be made only to produce a pure sound....

"Furthermore, bodily consciousness, which is directly reflected in figural sculpture, is transmuted by the sacred dance: the Hindu sculptor must know the rules of the sacred dance, which is the first of the figurative arts, since it has man himself as its means. Sculpture is thus related to two radically different arts: by its artisanal technique it is related to architecture, which is essentially static and transforms time into space, whereas the dance is essentially dynamic and transforms space into time, by absorbing the former into the continuity of rhythm. It is therefore not surprising that these two poles of Hindu art — sculpture and dancing — should have together engendered what is perhaps the most perfect fruit of Hindu art, the image of Shiva dancing.

"The dance of Shiva expresses at once the production, conservation, and destruction of the world, considered as phases of the permanent activity of God. Shiva is the 'Lord of the Dance' (*Natarâjâ*). He himself revealed the principles of the sacred dance to the sage Bharatamuni, who codified them in the *Bharata-Nâtya-Shâstra.**

"The static laws of sculpture and the rhythm of the dance are combined to perfection in the classical statue of Shiva dancing. The movement is conceived as a rotation around a motionless axis; by its decomposition into four typical gestures, following one another like phases, it reposes so to speak in its own amplitude; it is in no way rigid, but its rhythm is contained in a static formula, like the waves of liquid in a vessel; time is integrated in the timeless. The limbs of the God are arranged in such a way that the worshiper who views the statue from in front grasps

*"The 'celestial' origin of Hindu art is indirectly proved by its extension in space and time: in a form adapted to Buddhism, it has influenced the choreographic style of Tibet and all eastern Asia including Japan; in Java it survived the Islamicization of the island; and through the medium of Gypsy dancing it seems even to have influenced Spanish dancing."

all the forms at a glance: they are inscribed in the plane of the flaming circle, symbol of *Prakriti* (Universal Substance), without their spatial polyvalence being in any way impaired. On the contrary, from whatever side one contemplates the statue, its static equilibrium remains perfect, like that of a tree outspread in space. The plastic precision of the detail is combined with the uninterrupted continuity of the gestures.

"Shiva dances on the vanquished demon of chaotic matter, the subjective equivalent of which is spiritual indifference or forgetfulness of God (*apasmâra*). In his outermost right hand he holds the drum whose beat corresponds to the creative act. By the gesture of his uplifted hand he announces peace, protecting what he has created. His lowered hand points to the foot which is lifted from the ground, as a sign of deliverance. In his outermost left hand he carries the flame which will destroy the world.

"Images of Shiva dancing show sometimes the attributes of a god, sometimes those of an ascetic, or of both together, for God is beyond all forms, and He assumes form only so that He may become his own victim."

Titus Burckhardt,
Sacred Art in East and West, pages 37-39.

Shiva Natarâjâ
(Bronze statue, 11th century, Department of National
Museums, Colombo. Photograph: Nihal Fernando.)

It is the dharma *of water to flow, of fire to burn, of fish to swim, of birds to fly, and of man to achieve salvation.*

(29) Select Bibliography

Brockington, J. L., *The Sacred Thread — Hinduism in its Continuity and Diversity*, Edinburgh University Press, 1981.

Burckhardt, Titus, "The Genesis of the Hindu Temple" in *Sacred Art of East and West*, Perennial Books, London, 1967.

Coomaraswamy, Ananda, *Hinduism and Buddhism*, Philosophical Library, New York, 1943.

———— *The Religious Basis of the Forms of Indian Society*, Orientalia, New York, 1946.

———— *Spiritual Authority and Temporal Power in the Indian Theory of Government*, American Oriental Society, New Haven, Conn., 1942.

Eck, Diana L., *Darśan — Seeing the Divine Image in India*, Anima Books, Chambersburg, Pennsylvania, 2nd edition, 1985.

———— *Banaras, City of Light*, Alfred Knopf, New York, 1982.

Guénon, René, *Introduction to the Study of the Hindu Doctrines*, Luzac, London, 1945.

———— *Man and his becoming according to the Vedânta*, Luzac, London, 1945.

———— *Études sur l'Hindouisme*, Les Éditions Traditionnelles, Paris, 1968 and 1973.

Hopkins, Thomas J., *The Hindu Religious Tradition*, Dickinson, Encino, Calif., 1971.

Iengar, Keshavram and Dutt, K. Guru, *Notes on Hindu Dharma*, duplicated by Hebbar & Co., and privately published in the 1970s.

Kinsley, David R., *Hinduism: a cultural perspective*, Prentice Hall, Englewood Cliffs, N.J., 1982.

Klostermaier, Klaus K., *Survey of Hinduism*, State University of New York Press, Albany, 1989.

Lemaître, Solange, *Hinduism*, Hawthorn Books, New York, 1959.

Masui, Jacques (editor), *Approches de l'Inde*, Les Cahiers du Sud, Paris, 1949.

Morgan, Kenneth W. (editor), *The Religion of the Hindus*, The Ronald Press Company, N.Y., 1953.

Râmakrishna, Shrî, *The Gospel of Śri Ramakrishna*, recorded by Mahendranath Gupta, Ramakrishna — Vivekananda Center, New York, 1942.

Râmana Mahârshi, Shrî, *Talks with Sri Ramana Maharshi* (in 3 volumes), recorded by M. S. Venkataramiah, Ramanasramam, Tiruvannamalai, 1955.

Ramdas, Swami, *In Quest of God*, Anandashram, Kahangad, 1st edition 1925; many later editions, incl. Sivananda Press, Durban, 1979.

—— *In the Vision of God*, Anandashram, Kahangad, Kerala, 1950.

Schuon, Frithjof, "The Vedânta" in *Spiritual Perspectives*, Perennial Books, London, 1970.

—— "Modes de la réalisation spirituelle" in *L'Oeil du Coeur*, Dervy, Paris, 1974; English translation: "Modes of Spiritual Realization" in *Avaloka*, Vol. VI, Grand Rapids Michigan, 1992.

—— "A view of Yoga" in *Language of the Self*, Ganesh, Madras, 1959; 2nd edition, Sri Lanka, Institute of Traditional Studies, Colombo, 1992.

—— "The Meaning of Caste" in *Castes and Races*, Perennial Books, London, 1982.

—— "Mahâshakti" in *Roots of the Human Condition*, World Wisdom Books, Bloomington, Indiana, 1991.

Smith, Lee and Bodin, Wes (editors), *The Hindu Tradition*, Tabor Publishing, Valencia, California, 1978.

Vreede, Frans, *The Essentials of Living Hindu Philosophy*, Oxford University Press, London and Bombay, 1953.

Zimmer, Heinrich, *Myths and Symbols in Indian Art and Civilization*, Harper & Row, New York, 1962.

The highest mystery of the Vedanta, delivered in a former age, should not be taught to one whose passions have not been subdued, nor to one who is not a son or a pupil.

When these truths are taught to a man of good character — to a man who has the highest devotion for God, and for the Guru even as for God — then will they shine forth indeed.

Shvetâshvatara Upanishad, VI, 22-23.

Salutations to the glorious Guru, for the Guru is Brahmâ, the Guru is Vishnu, and even Lord Maheshvara (Shiva) is he. Verily, the Guru is the Supreme Brahman Himself.

The *Gurur Brahmâ* verse.

(30) Index of Sanscrit terms and proper names